Old KILCONQUHAR and CC

by
Eric Eunson

A traction engine belonging to A. & R. Brown of Colinsburgh photographed at Kilconquhar Station in the early 1920s. Alexander and Robert Brown started an agricultural engineering business at the east end of Main Street around 1900. The firm kept three sets of ploughing tackle and six of threshing plant for hire to local farms until the late 1920s. Traction engines were used to deliver and power the threshing machines, and were also employed to launch boats at the St Monans boatyards. Increasing ownership of tractors on local farms after 1918 reduced business considerably, although the powerful traction engines were still in demand for heavy haulage.

© Eric Eunson 2005
First published in the United Kingdom, 2005,
by Stenlake Publishing Ltd.
Telephone: 01290 551122
Printed by Cordfall Ltd., Glasgow, G21 2QA

ISBN 1 84033 345 6

**The publishers regret that they cannot supply
copies of any pictures featured in this book.**

For full details of all books currently available from
Stenlake Publishing, and to order copies, please visit
www.stenlake.co.uk. (If you would prefer a printed list and
order form please phone or write to us.) All orders to UK
addresses are **post-free**, and books can be despatched
worldwide for a small flat-rate charge.

Stenlake Publishing Ltd.,
54–58 Mill Square, Catrine, Ayrshire, Scotland, KA5 6RD.
phone +44 (0)1290 551122
www.stenlake.co.uk

INTRODUCTION

The villages covered in this book are contained within the Parish of Kilconquhar, and this brief account of their history cannot begin without a glance at the history of the parish itself. At different times both villages have enjoyed importance vastly disproportionate to their size: Kilconquhar as a religious centre, and Colinsburgh as an economic one. In both cases the significance of the villages has been directly affected by the proximity of major estates, and a summary of the history of these is also essential to the story of the villages.

The Parish of Kilconquhar was, and is, by far one of the largest in Fife. It is bounded by the sea on its southern fringe, and reaches eight miles inland to Largoward in the north, averaging two miles in width. Until the seventeenth century it included the Parish of Elie, devolved in 1639, and St Monans or Inverie, which was united with David Leslie's Barony of Newark and integrated into Abercrombie Parish in 1646. Kilconquhar also formerly embraced Earlsferry, conjoined with Elie parochially and administratively in 1890.

The origin of the name Kilconquhar is generally thought to derive from the presence of a 'kil' or cell of a holy man named Conacher. No legend of his life has survived, but it is possible that he was a Culdee, a sect of the old Celtic church which flourished in Fife between the eighth and twelfth centuries. However, Conacher may be a corruption of Cainneach, anglicised to St Kenneth, who died in AD 600 and is said to have founded the church at Kilrymont, forerunner of St Andrews Cathedral. If this theory is correct it would go a long way to explaining the religious importance of Kilconquhar Parish, for it was a very holy place. Balcarres was 'Balnacrois', the town of the cross, and just inside the neighbouring parish of Newburn is Balchrystie, the town of the Christians, an important Culdee settlement founded in the second half of the eleventh century.

The earliest mention of Kilconquhar Church dates from a stipendiary list of 1177, when it commanded the highest salary of the thirteen churches then in existence between Crail and Kennoway. With a stipend of 100 merks, it topped even Crail (80 merks), then a major religious and royal centre. Included with the church was a chapel, assumed to be the Chapel of Our Lady of Rires, which was located near the present-day Rires Farm on the Balcarres estate.

The first recorded owner of the Kilconquhar estate was Odo de Kilconcath, noted in 1200. His grandson Adam de Kilconcath is mentioned in 1250 as a close companion of 'Robert de Brus' in the sixth Crusade. Adam perished at Acco in Palestine in 1270, in the arms of de Brus, having previously acquired the title of Earl of Carrick through his marriage to Marjorie, the heiress of that line. When Bruce returned to Scotland he visited his friend's widow to impart the news of his death. Whirlwind romance blossomed, and fifteen days later they were married, with De Brus acquiring the titles of Earl of Carrick and Laird of Kilconquhar into the bargain. The son of this union was that most famous of Scottish kings, Robert the Bruce.

Rires was the principal estate of the parish, and from an unknown date formed part of the vast fiefdom of the Earls of Fife. In 1293–4 it was described as the 'Schyra de Ryrays' and comprised the lands of Balnacrois, the mill of the same name, the towns of Wester Ryrys (sic) and Balneil, the arable farm of Ryrys, and the workshop and coal pits on that farm (a very early reference to coal working in Fife at a location that was still being mined over 600 years later). The Chapel of Our Lady was close to Rires Castle, of which little can now be discerned, although its 70-foot boundary ditch could still be traced at the end of the eighteenth century.

By the mid-fourteenth century Rires was in the hands of David Wemyss. In 1393 he received a charter to build a 'castle with turrets', indicating a rebuilding of the earlier fortalice. In 1477 the estate passed to Arthur Forbes through his marriage to Elizabeth Wemyss.

The subsequent break-up of the estate cannot be summarised easily, as it relates to most of the estates of Lathallan, Balcarres and Charleton. Of these, Balcarres is the most important to the story as it concerns the foundation of Colinsburgh. In 1581 Balcarres passed via marriage to John Lindsay, Lord Menmuir, first of the Lindsays of Balcarres. He erected the first part of Balcarres House in 1595. During the seventeenth century the lordship of Balcarres included the lands of Balneil, Balcarres and Mill of Balcarres, Nether Cummerlands, Balboothie, Easter and Wester Pitcorthie, Balmakim and Nether Rires. John's eldest son, also John Lindsay, died in 1601 and the estate passed to his younger son, Sir David Lindsay. He was an Episcopalian sympathiser, but when Charles I attempted to introduce the Scottish service book, he went over to the Covenanters. His son Alexander was also a Covenanter and led troops at the battles of Alford and Kilsyth in 1645.

Charles II was crowned at Scone in 1651 and subsequently travelled through Fife bestowing honours, often courting his father's former enemies. The political expediency of winning friends explains the apparent paradox of his awarding Alexander Lindsay the title of Earl of Balcarres the same year. Charles was intent on raising a Scottish army to restore him to the throne, and Lindsay raised troops and marched to Worcester with them in 1651. He survived the Royalist defeat, but spent the remainder of his life in exile in Europe, dying in 1659, only months before the Restoration of Charles II.

Colin Lindsay, 3rd Earl of Balcarres, was born in 1652. In 1688 James II was deposed and fled into European exile. Lord Balcarres remained loyal to the old king and suffered imprisonment and a period of exile, returning to Scotland in 1700. He participated in the rebellion of 1715 and was leniently punished, being placed under guard but allowed to see out his days in the comfort of Balcarres.

In 1681 Colin bought the portion of Rires called Nether Rires from Sir William Bruce of Balcaskie, who had held it only briefly. The following year he granted three feus, and this is generally accepted as the date of the foundation of Colinsburgh, although a scattered hamlet already existed at Nether Rires by 1649 when it was home to seven families. Two years earlier Margaret Tailyour is recorded as being keeper of an alehouse in Nether Rires, one of four in the parish, and in 1680 a blacksmith is also noted. The earl gave the village the name Colinsburgh in 1686, and it was elevated to the status of burgh of barony the same year. This entitled its occupants to hold weekly fairs – which took place on a Tuesday – and two annual eight-day fairs, one commencing on the first Friday in June and the other taking place from 4 October. The development of these made Colinsburgh the principal market town for a wide rural area. The fairs flourished for a century and a half, but then went into decline and had all but ceased by the 1860s.

Tradition maintains that Lord Balcarres founded Colinsburgh to house his disbanded Jacobite troops, but it seems more likely that an unplanned influx of former soldiers accounted for a concentration of feus granted between 1706 and 1721. The farmhouse at the top of North Wynd was built in 1717, and was later occupied by John Fair, estate factor, who named it Fairfield after himself. The associated barn dates from 1734, and together these were undoubtedly the most substantial farm buildings in east Fife in this period. Most of the feus giving Colinsburgh its present dimensions were granted before the close of the eighteenth century.

The 1700s marked an era of great progress in Scotland, notably in agriculture, with field enclosure and improved drainage widespread by 1750. Many people are surprised to discover how many vegetables that we now take for granted were newly introduced around this time. The Earl of Balcarres planted field turnips on his farms around 1750, and Swedish turnips were first grown there in the 1780s. The 1792 *Statistical Account* of the parish states that potatoes, almost unknown in the parish in 1750, by then afforded the poor half their sustenance, and were widely used as animal fodder, besides being distilled into whisky.

A post office had been established in Colinsburgh by 1755, then one of only fourteen in the whole county, the others being confined to major towns. It remained the only post office between Leven and Pittenweem until another was opened at Elie in 1797, and this may be taken as an indicator of the importance of the village at this time.

In 1792 the village populations were as follows: Colinsburgh 357; Kilconquhar 258; and Barnyards 198. The country part of the parish contained 850 people, indicating that agriculture was by far the most important part of the economy, although mining must also have employed a significant number of people, perhaps 200. At this time coal was being wrought at several places in the north of the parish: at Rires; North and South Falfield; Kilbrackmont; Lathallan; and Largoward.

There were no fewer than 46 shoemakers in the parish in 1792, but only four by 1825. In 1792 it was reported that 89 were employed in weaving. By 1837 this number had increased to 235, when it was noted that the industry was entirely confined to the villages, there being not a single weaver in the landward area. The population of Colinsburgh had increased to 561 between these two dates, with that of Kilconquhar and Barnyards growing from 456 to 558. Both Colinsburgh and Kilconquhar were to remain predominantly agricultural villages for another century, but by the 1950s mechanisation meant that most small farms needed only one or two men to work them. Both villages saw an increasing number of young people moving where employment lay: local shops closed and the population grew more grey haired. In 1951 Kilconquhar was described as 'virtually moribund' and continued to decline and decay into the 1960s. However, within a decade it had been utterly transformed by sensitive restoration, although its function today is largely that of a retirement and commuter settlement. In 1999 the population of Colinsburgh was estimated at 389 and that of Kilconquhar 261.

As I write it is almost 25 years to the day since I moved with my parents into the Corner House shop at the corner of South Wynd, which we ran for five years. I hope local people will not be too critical of this slim volume, and will make allowances for the omissions of a one-time 'incomer'.

Railway Station, Kilconquhar.

67786 J.V

Proposals for a railway from Markinch or Thornton to Anstruther were put forward in 1845, with stations at or near Colinsburgh and Kilconquhar. Styled the East of Fife Railway, the plans were too ambitious and never made it beyond the prospectus stage. Some years later, between 1852 and 1854, the Leven Railway was constructed from Thornton to Leven with proposals to extend the line to Kilconquhar ratified in 1855. The extension went ahead and a special inaugural train ran to Kilconquhar Station on 31 July 1857, the line officially opening on 11 August. The renamed Leven & East of Fife Railway was extended to Anstruther in 1863. This postcard of Kilconquhar Station dates from 1909. Today only the stationmaster's house remains, the roof of which can be seen on the left.

The 2.10 p.m. from Dundee to Edinburgh pictured at Kilconquhar Station on 22 April 1957. The fork on the right was a siding for goods, and beyond it the St Ford farmhouse can be glimpsed. All stations between Leven and St Andrews were closed on 6 September 1965. One of the last vestiges of the old station was a level crossing gate adjacent to the Shell Bay road which lasted into the 1980s, but this has now gone. *Photograph © W. A. C. Smith.*

Parish Church Manse, Kilconquhar.

Until 1717 the manse for Kilconquhar Parish was located in Earlsferry. In that year the proprietor of Elie estate donated land at Kilconquhar to the church in exchange for the existing glebe at Earlsferry, which he bequeathed to the kirk session of Elie for the poor of the parish. The manse in this 1920s picture was designed in 1814–15 by local architect and wright Alexander Leslie. It was extensively remodelled in 1851–2 by George Just, who lowered the pitch of the roof and rebuilt the facade. The property was sold by the Church of Scotland some years ago.

As mentioned in the introduction, a church is first noted at Kilconquhar in 1177, but there is every reason to suppose that one had existed on the site for several centuries beforehand. Some sources have suggested the 1177 church may have superseded a pre-Christian place of worship, and this is highly likely as early churches were often founded on existing religious sites. In 1200, Duncan, Earl of Fife, gifted Kilconquhar Church to the Convent of North Berwick, and this grant was confirmed by his son Malcolm in 1228. In 1499 there is a record of a donation by Patrick Dunbar to 'the altar of our Lady of Pete (Pity)' in Kilconquhar Parish Church. The parish was provided with a Protestant minister in 1565, and in 1577 William Bellenden is noted as being the vicar. During the religious conflicts of the seventeenth century the parish was universally on the side of the Covenanters, and the Covenant was sworn here in 1643 and 1648. James Drummond, minister of Kilconquhar, was imprisoned in 1674 for preaching conventicles in private houses, and again in 1677 when he was sent to the formidable prison on the Bass. Large illegal assemblies gathered on Balcarres Crag to hear the words of Covenanting preachers. In 1681 two Kilconquhar weavers, Adam Philip and Lawrence Hay, along with Andrew Pittilloch, a labourer from Earlsferry, were executed for publishing a propagandist Covenanting paper entitled *Testimony Against the Evils of the Times*, although they had done no more than sign their names to it. Their severed heads were displayed on the tollbooth at Cupar, and a memorial stone marks the spot where these were buried in Cupar kirkyard. In the eighteenth century a new spirit of religious tolerance prevailed, and this led to the growth of a plethora of sects. A Relief congregation was established in Colinsburgh in 1760, and by 1837 there were three other dissenting churches in the parish: a second Relief church in Colinsburgh, a United Associate Synod, and an Independent church. In addition there was a Baptist meeting house. Despite the variety of options on offer, there were only 361 dissenters in the parish, and the Revd William Ferrie remarked pithily 'What stipends these ministers receive is not known. They must be very small.' Kilconquhar Church was rebuilt in 1819–21 by R. & R. Dickson using Richard Crichton's 1818 design for Cockpen Church near Dalkeith. The two buildings appear almost identical. The present pulpit was a memorial to the Revd Alex and Mrs Legge, installed in 1921, and the baptismal font dates from 1924. In 1935 the churches of Colinsburgh and Kilconquhar were united under a single minister, the Revd R. S. Armstrong, and Kilconquhar Kirk was lit by electricity for the first time in the same year. Declining attendances led to a further merger of the two kirks with Elie Church in 1986.

This atmospheric view of Kilconquhar dates from 1921. The trees on the right-hand side of the churchyard were removed many years ago, and the adjacent field was used to extend the cemetery in the 1970s. The building on the left adjoining the Kinneuchar Inn was rebuilt in 1968.

Kilconquhar Kirk and Loch on a wintry day in 1880, photographed by Valentine of Dundee. The building on the right was a tannery owned by David Carstairs of Colinsburgh, who also carried out a thriving currier's business in his home town on the site of what is now Magnus Dunsire's joinery workshop. In 1825 it was described as 'the principal establishment of the place', and in 1837 it was said to manufacture leather with a value of £14–15,000 per annum, providing employment for between twenty and 24 men at a wage of around £15 a year. Despite its seeming success, the business had been abandoned by 1867 and the tannery was left to decay. The neighbouring white cottages in the picture have also long gone.

The old arches to the rear of the kirk are all that remains of Kilconquhar's pre-Reformation church. When it was being taken down in 1819–20 it was discovered that the original foundations both outside and inside the building were over a dozen feet below ground level, such was the build-up of centuries of burials, and a vast quantity of bones was removed. Near here is a recumbent figure of a helmeted knight, minus his feet and badly worn. He has been nicknamed 'Jock o' Balclevie', recalling a lost hamlet on the Elie estate, but he was almost certainly one of the lairds of Kilconquhar.

'They shall not grow old, as we who are left grow old.' Solemn faces on the sombre occasion of the unveiling of Kilconquhar war memorial on 25 September 1921.

Main Street, Kilconquhar, looking east from the road to Colinsburgh, 1905. When the pair of ashlar houses (built *c.*1850) in the foreground developed an alarming bulge in the front wall they were demolished, with houses of similar dimensions erected on the site in 2004. The cottage and two-storey house in the middle distance were demolished in the 1960s and replaced by Conacher Court. Further up the street the building with its gable facing the camera was the home and shop of William Thomson, grocer, which was nicknamed 'the Klondyke', allegedly because Mr Thomson had made a modest fortune in the Canadian gold rush.

KILCONQUHAR SCHOOL AND BARNYARDS FROM THE CHURCH TOWER.

2133.

The first parochial schoolmaster of Kilconquhar was Sir William Galland (the 'sir' is an ecclesiastical title), referred to in 1593. In 1695 the kirk session proposed the allocation of £230 to erect a school and schoolhouse. The *Statistical Account* of 1792 alludes only to the parish school, but a reference of 1799 mentions four 'adventure' schools in the parish. These were not offering a more exciting curriculum – the adventure was whether the teacher could make them pay! Exact dates are often hard to establish for the construction of school buildings as they tended to evolve without much notice in records, and that of Kilconquhar is no exception. This view of Kilconquhar School dates from *c.*1930. It was closed in the summer of 1980, when there was some talk of using it as a community centre, but in 1984 it was converted into housing with additional development in the grounds.

Kilconquhar Church seen from the east in 1909. The cottage on the left belonged to an Irishman named Lukie Malaney, and was demolished *c.*1920 to make way for the war memorial. A drawing of Kilconquhar in 1830 shows two cottages actually in the churchyard, surrounded by gravestones. An old Colinsburgh gentleman told me it was a favourite prank of local lads to lift a divot from the kirkyard and put it on Lukie's chimney before waiting for the irate householder to emerge in a cloud of smoke.

One can almost hear the buzz of the bees from Lukie's rose garden in this summery 1910 view. New occupants are arriving at the house on the left, preceded by rolls of linoleum. The picturesque scene belies the primitive conditions behind the facades. Many houses in the village still drew water from wells in 1951, but it was remarked that the poor housing did provide property at low rents for the elderly. A resident once told me that £100 would have bought the whole village at the time, and I have heard it told that a cottage in Barnyards changed hands for £5 in a private bargain. A far cry from the telephone number property prices here today!

Kilconquhar from the Church Tower, looking East.

This panoramic view of Main Street is postmarked 1932 and shows Bella Ramsay's cottage in the right foreground. Kilconquhar Loch is the remnant of a vast lake created by melting glaciers around 10,000 years ago. Tradition maintains that it once had an outlet to the sea which was blocked by drifting sand after a huge storm in 1624. It was formerly known as Redmire, and in 1792 it was remarked that it had formerly yielded much fuel for the villagers in the form of peats. Reeds for thatch are not mentioned, probably because at the time their benefit would have been too obvious to merit remarking.

KILCONQUHAR.

85417 J.V.

The 'bullnose' Morris tourer belonged to the photographer of this 1921 view, which shows Kilconquhar post office on the right. This opened on 1 June 1854 as a sub-office of Colinsburgh, at which time letters were marked on the reverse using an undated 'Kilconquhar' name-stamp before being transferred to Colinsburgh where the stamp was cancelled and a date-stamp applied. Kilconquhar post office closed on 1 April 1970, way ahead of sweeping rural office cuts. With it went the last shop in the village, which has since also lost its school and public hall.

Main Street 100 years ago seen on a picture postcard published by Lewis Cameron, the Colinsburgh pharmacist. His imprint appears on a couple of dozen local views by Valentine of Dundee and George Washington Wilson of Aberdeen. Today people are astonished that so many postcards were once produced of such diminutive places as Kilconquhar and Colinsburgh, but in the first quarter of last century mail deliveries were far more frequent – twice a day in most villages and up to six times a day in the cities. Postcards served the same function that the telephone does now, and Edwardian examples frequently carry messages informing of a visit 'this afternoon'.

KILCONQUHAR, LOOKING WEST

85545 J.V.

An evening shower – note the long shadows – has doubtless cleared the air in this 1921 scene. Little has changed, except that the road was tarred in the late 1930s and the post office was complemented by a 'Jubilee' phone box, which still remains, around the same time. The meanly proportioned cottages on the right were combined into larger homes when they were restored in the early 1970s, but retain their character with fewer doorways.

The east end of the village in 1909, showing the smiddy on the left. No blacksmith is noted in Kilconquhar in 1825, but in 1837 George Morgan is listed in *Pigot's Directory*, while in 1867 two smiths are noted in the village, George Greig and George Izett.

Curling on Kilconquhar Loch in 1904. In 1895 the Hercules Ladies' Club was instituted with twenty members, making it the first ladies' curling club in Scotland. The Kilconquhar Juniors Club was instituted in 1835, and being largely composed of Colinsburgh men was reorganised as the Colinsburgh Club in 1893. The Hercules clubhouse was destroyed by fire a couple of years ago, with the loss of all club records and many irreplaceable items of memorabilia.

The popularity of curling in the district is testament to the harshness of winters in earlier centuries. Every local estate had an artificial rink, with one located in the north-west corner of the public playing field at Colinsburgh. The sender of this 1904 postcard comments 'Once a traction engine went over this loch after sixteen weeks hard frost'. Except, of course, he has got the location wrong, as this is not the loch but the area behind the Kinneuchar Inn, showing Barnyards in the background. The figure in the centre of the picture with the wide brimmed hat is believed to be the Revd Alexander Legge.

VIEW IN BARNYARDS, KILCONQUHAR
85551 J.V.

The passage of over 80 years has scarcely altered this 1921 picture of Barnyards. There is a tendency among local history writers to blithely call all single-storey houses 'weavers cottages', as though weaving necessitated a particular type of house. During the development of more efficient farms from c.1750 many people were ejected from subsistence crofts and took up trades in nearby villages, which correspondingly grew in the same period. The handloom weaving industry boomed from c.1790–1840, enabling many weavers to afford to have substantial cottages built. Barnyards was largely feued in this half-century.

In 1837 it was stated that 235 people were employed in weaving in Kilconquhar Parish, 120 men and 115 women. The raw materials were generally obtained from manufacturers in Kirkland (by Leven), Kirkcaldy and Dundee. These same manufacturers employed agents to buy the finished articles, including 'dowlasses, checks and sheetings'. The cottages on the right of this 1909 picture have been replaced by sympathetic 1970s housing.

In 1390 the Kilconquhar estate was owned by George Dunbar, Earl of March and Dunbar. It remained in the Dunbar family until the last heir, Andrew Dunbar, died without issue in 1564. The estate was then purchased by Sir John Bellenden, whose descendants held it until 1634, when it was bought by Sir John Carstares (sic). In 1714 it was acquired by Thomas Beton of Tarvit. The mansion house was built for Sir Henry Beton (or Bethune, which became the preferred spelling) in 1831–9. He was created a baronet in 1836 for his services in Persia, and died in Teheran in 1851. This view of Kilconquhar House from the north was taken in 1904. A single-storey extension was added to the left of the entrance in 1915.

Kilconquhar House from the south in 1909. The mansion was designed by William Burn in baronial style, incorporating an existing seventeenth century tower house, which can be seen on the left . The estate was sold in the 1970s with the house intended to be the centrepiece of a timeshare development. A devastating fire in 1978 destroyed the interior and forced the immediate demolition of the south facade on the right of the picture. Only the extension of 1915 survived intact, and this became the 'Bunker Bar' and 'Lindsay Room' of so-called Kilconquhar Castle, a somewhat grandiose name for a dishevelled Victorian ruin. It was reconstructed after a fashion in the 1980s, with the old tower cut down and the addition of a new facade which bears no relation to the original.

MUIRCAMBUS.

Newly completed farm cottages at Muircambus, photographed in 1907. *Cam* in Celtic means crooked, and Muircambus probably takes its name from the windings of the Cocklemill Burn. In 1452 the estate was listed as being among the possessions of St Andrews Cathedral. It passed through a complex succession of proprietors until it was sold to Sir William Scott of Elie in the late sixteenth century, remaining part of Elie estate until 1812 when the northern part was sold to John Fortune, who erected the present mansion house.

CHARLETON HOUSE, COLINSBURGH.

200,313.JV.

The estate of Charleton includes Wester Rires, and Easter and Wester Newton Rires, which subsequently became known simply as Newton. Wester Newton Rires was acquired by John Thomson of Charleton in 1740, and it is he who changed the name. The first part of Charleton House was a plain rectangular block, built for John Thomson in 1749. Wings to the rear were added by Alexander Leslie in 1815–17, and the dining room on the right of the photograph was built by William Burn in 1832. Robert S. Lorimer made minor alterations to the exterior in the 1900s, and extensively remodelled the interior. The layout of the garden also dates from the Edwardian period. This photograph was taken in 1926.

A travelling draper attracts customers in this *c*.1900 view of the west end of Main Street, Colinsburgh. In the early eighteenth century nearly all the households in Colinsburgh had a portion of land of between one and three acres outside the village. All the roadside land between Charleton and Balcarres Mill (at the entrance to Cairnie House) was taken up by these crofts, which were used for sowing grain or grazing cattle. As the original feuars' lines died out, these crofts reverted to Balcarres estate.

MAIN STREET, COLINSBURGH.

This view dates from 1925 and shows the Masonic hall on the right. In 1923 a fund-raising bazaar at Balcarres House raised £1,050 towards the cost of the building. Lodge Balcarres, No. 1,240, was formally opened on 26 July 1924. Earlier trade societies had flourished in the area, and at the start of the nineteenth century there were groups of 'Apron Men' (a guild which admitted young men at the close of their apprenticeships) in both villages, while the Free Gardeners had a hall in South Wynd. The publisher of this postcard evidently thought Colinsburgh not busy enough (it isn't noted for its bustle) and added figures and a rather out of scale motor car to liven up the scene!

Main Street has hardly changed since this 1909 photograph was taken. The Galloway Library on the left was designed in 1903 by Charles Davidson of Paisley, and has been variously described as 'suety' and 'municipal pomposity'. It is a little overdone, but it does relieve the stern elevation of the street. The Balcarres Arms Hotel, opposite, was called the New Inn in 1823 and was known as the Plough in 1837. The first innkeeper was Mrs Elizabeth Ronald, who was also postmistress, so it is safe to say that the post office was located in the inn. By 1867, when Robert Maw was proprietor, it had become the Balcarres Arms. To the west of where the library stands there was formerly a stream across the road called the Water Gate, crossed by a wooden bridge, but it was culverted into the village drains in 1886.

Main Street, Colinsburgh.

63821 J.V.

This 1909 view tells much of its own story. The postcard was bought from the man in the left foreground, Lewis Cameron the chemist, and posted across the road in the post office run by John Niven. On the latter's death in 1935 the post office moved into Cameron's chemist's shop. Colinsburgh Church, on the right, was founded in 1760 as a Relief church, and it is recorded that as many as 1,500 people previously took communion there, coming from as far afield as Crail and Dysart. The present church replaced the dilapidated building of 1760 in 1843. In 1847 the Secession and Relief Churches united to become the United Presbyterian Church.

MAIN STREET, COLINSBURGH

B 8192

The house with the bay window on the right of this 1953 picture was built around 1905 on a site first feued to Colin Bennet, vintner, in 1682. Cameron's chemist's shop, beyond, stands on a feu of the same age. The first houses in Colinsburgh were erected on the north side of Main Street, west of North Wynd, which marked the boundary between Nether Rires and the Balcarres estate. The building two doors down from Cameron's stands on a site feued to William Kinloch in 1687, and in 1896 was described as a double house, one half of which was in ruins. One feature of this 1953 scene locals would dearly like to change is the overhead power lines, a continuing cause of power cuts and thawing freezers to this day.

A Masonic parade turning into South Wynd in the 1920s, possibly on the occasion of the opening of the Masonic hall in 1924. The three-storey building on the right stands on the first feu east of the wynd, and the first outside the Nether Rires lands, which was granted in 1687. The feu directly opposite was granted the same year. It was long in the hands of the Skinner family, and Mrs Elizabeth Skinner is noted as a grocer and hardware dealer in 1825. The last of the Skinners were two elderly spinsters, and when the second of them died in the 1950s a local man related how he was offered the entire property, complete with contents, for a mere £50! The building was altered in the 1930s when the present large windows were installed.

The premises of Thomas Aitken the plumber are on the right of this 1910 view taken in South Wynd, then called Station Road. The upper flat of the neighbouring two-storey house served as a meeting place for the Free Gardeners, a society similar to the Freemasons, although no mention of the Colinsburgh Lodge could be traced in any records of the order extant in 1896. The United Presbyterian congregation worshipped in this flat while their new church was under construction in 1843, and it long served the village as a public hall. Next door to these buildings was the former gasworks, founded in 1841 as the Colinsburgh Gas Light Company, making gas from coal. A lovely cast iron lamp set on top of the wall on the west side of the wynd is the last relic of this progressive enterprise.

The house second from the left of this 1902 view was formerly the United Presbyterian Church manse. Two Colinsburgh ministers wrote books on the area. In 1883 Revd Robert Dick published his *History of Colinsburgh UP Church*, a limited edition of 100 copies, all of which were sold within six weeks. He went on to write the *Annals of Colinsburgh* in 1896, a superb reference from which I have borrowed considerably. In 1932 Revd John Adams wrote *Balcarres Crag*, a charming book of natural history. Three of the houses on the right were demolished in the 1960s to create the forecourt of Andersons' garage and filling station. This closed down some years ago, and new houses were built on the site in 2004.

The house on the left of this 1909 postcard view is now attached to the remaining filling station in the village. In the late 1970s a price war raged between the two garages on opposite sides of the street, and Colinsburgh became a regular detour for drivers who knew it had the cheapest petrol in east Fife. Fairfield Road now branches off to the left. The local authority completed its first scheme of houses here in 1939, and the second phase was reported as under construction in 1951. The two-storey house beyond the town hall was home to Alexander Brown, agricultural engineer. His adjacent works was destroyed by fire in 1931, and by the time the Buckhaven and Cupar brigades had the blaze under control £5,000 worth of damage had been caused. Alexander Brown Snr died in 1921 aged 92; his son Alexander died in 1950 aged 86.

Town Hall, Colinsburgh.

63818. JV.

Bazaars were held in the grounds of Balcarres House in 1882 and 1893 for the purpose of rasing money to provide Colinsburgh with a public hall. The building was erected in 1894, partly on the site of a sewing school belonging to Lady Lindsay. The architect was A. C. Dewar, the Leven town council burgh surveyor, and it was formally opened on 25 October 1895 by the Earl of Crawford. The town hall continues to be well-used by local groups, and is the venue for one of the high spots in the local calendar, the annual Colinsburgh & Kilconquhar Horticultural Society show, the first of which was held in August 1936. An earlier horticultural society was founded in 1865 but seems to have been wound up c.1895.

Golden Gates, Colinsburgh.

63819 J.V.

The South Lodge was erected in 1871, when Sir Coutts Lindsay created a new approach to Balcarres House. During the digging of the foundations of the lodge, workmen unearthed several coffins made from stone slabs. The bodies they contained were buried in a sitting posture, typical of Bronze Age 'short cist' graves of *c*.2,500 BC, and when Dr Kennedy of Elie examined one of the thigh bones he deduced it must have belonged to an individual seven feet tall. The 'Golden Gates' were wrought in Cremona *c*.1700, and had to be fished from the seabed when the ship bringing them to Scotland sank. They were discreetly stored during the scrap iron drive of the Second World War.

This rare engraving of Balcarres House from the south-west dates from 1811. Part of Lord Menmuir's original house, begun in 1595, can be seen on the left and is still discernible today. The bow-fronted section was added in 1809 by the Hon. Robert Lindsay, who had purchased the estate from his brother, Alexander, Earl of Balcarres, in 1789. This separated the estate and title. Robert Lindsay was responsible for the planting of many trees in the park around the house c.1800, and it was he who began planting on the then barren Balcarres Crag. The folly on the crag was built in 1813 by James Fisher, wright. East Lodge, at the top of the Double Dykes Road, dates from 1794. This road was originally part of the public road from Lathallan to Colinsburgh, constructed in 1774, and the lodge originally formed the main entrance to the house.

Balcarres House, Colinsburgh, from N.E.

JV 63829

The sixteenth century part of the house is clearly discernible in the centre of this 1909 view, its sandstone being much lighter in colour than the surrounding whin. The portion on the right dates from William Burn's massive remodelling of the house, executed in 1838–43 for James Lindsay, a colonel of the Grenadier Guards and former MP for East Fife. The turreted section on the left dates from a further enlargement of the house in 1863–67 by David Bryce, famous for his baronial style. In 1886 Sir Coutts Lindsay, grandson of Hon. Robert Lindsay who bought the estate in 1789, sold Balcarres to his nephew, the Earl of Crawford and Balcarres, thus reuniting estate and title.

The Gardens, Balcarres House, Colinsburgh.

63825 J.V.

The south front of Balcarres showing William Burn's frontage, which replaced the Georgian bow fronted version shown on page 40. The upper terrace, with its balustraded wall, was built in 1841 and the double stairway added in the 1860s. The ornate flower beds and topiary had gone by the 1950s.

Local children lead a procession of 8th Argyll & Sutherland Highlanders on their way to camp at Largoward in July 1910. The building is the distinctive North Lodge of Balcarres House, known to locals as the 'De'il's Lodge' on account of the little grotesque perched on the rooftop. A local myth maintains that the sculptor modelled the 'De'il' on the then Earl of Crawford, who was tardy in settling his account. The lodge was designed by Scotland's most celebrated architect of the period, Robert S. Lorimer, in 1896–8, and is modelled on the sixteenth century Queen Mary's bathhouse near Holyrood.

Farm-workers cottages at Balneil *c.*1907. The name means simply 'Neil's town' and a township of sorts is noted here as part of the 'Schyra de Ryrays' in 1293.

Although scarcely a mile east of Colinsburgh, few locals have seen more than the rooftop of Cairnie House peeping above its densely wooded grounds. It was built in 1824 for the Misses Davidson. When the local volunteer yeomanry was founded in 1859, Walter Davidson of Cairnie was its lieutenant, and the success of the company was largely credited to his efforts. His son, Col. James Scott Davidson (1857–1913), and his wife were both keen curlers. Mrs Scott Davidson was one of the founders of the Hercules Ladies' Club, and Col. Davidson was a member of the first Scottish curling delegation to visit Canada and the United States in 1902. This picture dates from 1905.

AULD ROBIN GRAY'S COTTAGE, NEAR ELIE.

1153.

Auld Robin Gray's cottage seen in the 1920s, with Cairnie Home Farm cottages on the left. The road junction was staggered in the 1970s after several fatal accidents here. The song *The Ballad of Auld Robin Gray* was composed by Lady Anne Lindsay of Balcarres (1750–1825), the eldest daughter of James Lindsay, 5th Earl of Balcarres. It was written when she was 21, and is the only piece of writing attributed to her. At her insistence it was never published under her own name during her lifetime. The cottage in this picture was not the real home of Robin Gray, which is shown opposite.

Auld Robin Gray's cottage stood on the east side of the path through Balcarres Den, roughly in line with the entrance to Pitcorthie House. When this picture was taken in 1903 all that remained was the fragment of a gable, just discernible through the trees. Every author who mentions Colinsburgh refers to *The Ballad of Auld Robin Gray* knowing full-well that although it was a popular song for 200 years, very few people today know the words, so here they are:

Ruins of Auld Robin Gray's House

When the sheep are in the fauld, and the kye a' at hame
When a' the weary world to sleep are gane,
The waes o' my heart fall in showers frae my e'e,
While my gudeman lies sound by me.

Young Jamie lo'ed me weel, and sought me for his bride;
But saving a croun he had naethin' else beside.
To mak the croun an pound, my Jamie gaed to sea,
And the croun and the pound, they were baith for me.

He hadna been awa' a week but only twa,
When my mither she fell sick and the cow was stown awa';
My father brak his arm – my Jamie at the sea;
And Auld Robin Gray cam a – courtin' me.

My father couldna wark, my mither couldna spin,
I toil'd day and nicht, but their bread a couldna win;
Auld Rob maintain'd them baith, and wi tears in his e'e,
Said, 'Jeannie for their sakes, will ye marry me?'

My heart it said na – I'd look for Jamie back;
But the wind it blew hie, and the ship it was a wrack;
His ship it was a wrack – why didna Jamie dee?
And why do I live to cry, Wae's me?

My father urged me sair; my mither didna speak,
But she looked in my face till my heart was like to break.
They gied him my hand – my heart was at the sea;
Sae Auld Robin Gray, he was gudeman to me.

I hadna been a wife a week but only four,
When, mournfu' as I sat on the stane at the door,
I saw my Jamie's wraith – I couldna think it he,
Till he said,' I'm come hame my love, to marry thee.'

O sair did we greet, and meikle did we say:
We took but ae a kiss, and I bade him gang away.
I wish that I were dead, but I'm no like to dee;
And why was I born to say, Wae's me?

I gang like a ghaist, and I care na to spin;
I daurna think o' Jamie, for that wad be a sin.
But I'll do my best a gude wife to be,
For Auld Robin Gray, he is kind to me.

Pitcorthie House, east of Colinsburgh, photographed in 1909. The name is derived from the Celtic words *pette* and *coirthe* giving 'the town of the pillar stones', a plausible explanation as a fine standing stone decorated with cup marks is situated about half a mile to the east. Pitcorthie estate is noted way back in the eleventh century when it was the property of Siward, a Saxon noble who probably arrived with the entourage of St Margaret. The mansion was described by John Leighton in 1840 as 'recently erected', and as it is absent from both the *Statistical Account* and *Pigot's Directory* of 1837 this can be taken literally. It was built for James Simpson, but later became part of Balcarres estate. In 1926 the mansion was let to the Church of Scotland Young Men's Guild as a holiday home.